Rookie
Read-About®
Geography

by Rebecca Hi----

Content Consul
Roman Cybriwsk
Professor, Temple Univ

Reading Consultant
Jeanne Clidas
Reading Specialist

Children's Press®
An Imprint of Scholastic Inc.
New York • Toronto • London • Auckland • Sydney • Mexico City
New Delhi • Hong Kong • Danbury, Connecticut

Library of Congress Cataloging-in-Publication Data
Hirsch, Rebecca E.
  Asia / by Rebecca Hirsch ; content consultant, Roman Cybriwsky.
     p. cm. – (Rookie read-about geography)
  Includes index.
  ISBN 978-0-531-28977-8 (lib.bdg.) – ISBN 978-0-531-29277-8
(pbk.)
  1. Asia–Juvenile literature. 2. Asia–Geography–Juvenile
literature. I. Cybriwsky, Roman A. II. Title.

  DS5.H57 2012
  915–dc23

                    2012013399

SCHOLASTIC, CHILDREN'S PRESS, ROOKIE READ-ABOUT®,
and associated logos are trademarks and/or registered trademarks of
Scholastic Inc.

1 2 3 4 5 6 7 8 9 10 R 22 21 20 19 18 17 16 15 14 13

Photographs © 2013: age fotostock: 26, 31 bottom left (Christian Cueni/
Panther Media), 12 (Klaus-Werner Friedric/imagebroker), 22 (Tao
Images); Alamy Images: cover (Angelo Cavalli/Tips Images/Tips Italia Srl
a socio unico), 30 (dbimages); AP Images/Yuan Shuiling/Imaginechina:
10, 31 top right; Dreamstime/Pietrach: 8; Getty Images/Junko
Takahashi/a.collectionRF: 16; Shutterstock, Inc.: 29 (Kjersti Joergensen),
20, 31 bottom right (neelsky); Superstock, Inc.: 24, 31 top left (Blum
Bruno/Prisma), 14 (Hemis.fr), 4 (Steve Vidler), 18 (Wolfgang Kaehler).

Map by Matt Kania/www.maphero.com

Table of Contents

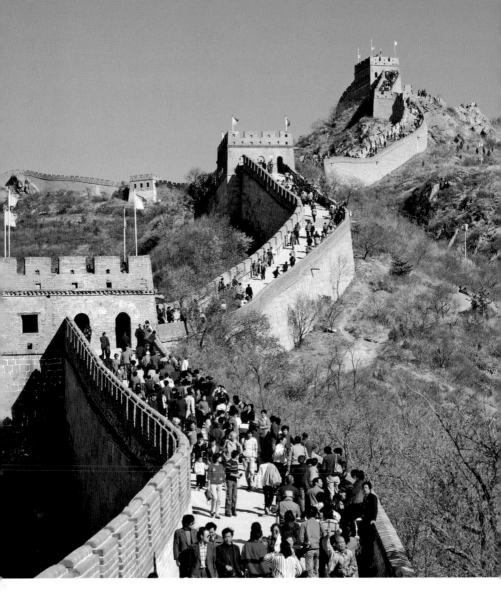

The Great Wall of China is in Asia.

Welcome to Asia!

Asia is the largest continent. It has more than 40 countries.

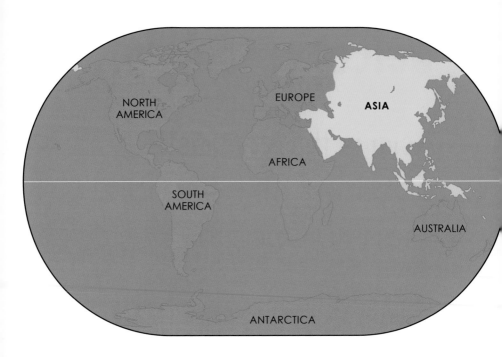

NORTH
AMERICA

EUROPE

ASIA

AFRICA

SOUTH
AMERICA

AUSTRALIA

ANTARCTICA

6

The largest pieces of land on Earth are continents. There are seven. Asia is the **yellow** continent on this map.

People shop at a street market in Mumbai, India.

People of Asia

Most of the world's people live in Asia. Some live in busy cities.

Workers build computer parts.

Many people work in modern factories. Most of the world's computer parts are made in Asia.

Women cleaning rice

Other people live in villages. They grow rice on farms. Most of the world's rice is from Asia.

Monsoon rains in Indonesia

Wild Weather

Asia has monsoons. These are strong winds. In summer, monsoons bring heavy rains.

A snowy day in Japan

Some parts of Asia have cold, snowy winters.

A giant panda eats bamboo.

Amazing Animals

Asia has lots of rare animals. Giant pandas live in Asia. Their favorite food is bamboo.

A Bengal tiger

Bengal tigers live in Asia's forests. Tigers are good hunters and like to swim.

Bamboo plants are tall.

Wild Places

Asia has forests. Some have many trees. Other forests grow bamboo plants.

Camels on the Gobi Desert

Asia has deserts.
The Gobi desert is dry.
Wind blows the sand
and makes dunes.

Mount Everest is windy and cold.

Mount Everest is in Asia. It is the tallest mountain on Earth. It is one of the many things that make Asia such a unique continent.

Modern Marvels

- The Burj Khalifa in Asia is the world's tallest building. It has 160 floors.

- The building took almost six years to build. It is made of steel, concrete, and glass.

- Some people live in the Burj Khalifa. Others work in the offices.

Try It!

What do people do in this building? Why do you think they used steel and concrete to build this building? If you made a tall building, what would it look like?

Meet a Komodo Dragon

- Komodo dragons are the biggest lizards in the world.

- They use their tongues to smell.

- They can use their claws to climb trees.

- Komodo dragons live on islands in Asia.

Words You Know

dunes

factory

mountain

tiger

Index

Facts for Now

Visit this Scholastic Web site for more information on Asia:
www.factsfornow.scholastic.com
Enter the keyword **Asia**

About the Author

Rebecca Hirsch is a scientist-turned-writer and the author of many books for young readers.

[5]